Pebble®

MATH

It's Subtraction!

by M. W. Penn

Consulting Editor: Gail Saunders-Smith, PhD

CAPSTONE PRESS
a capstone imprint

Pebble Books are published by Capstone Press,
1710 Roe Crest Drive, North Mankato, Minnesota, 56003.
www.capstonepub.com

Library of Congress Cataloging-in-Publication Data
Penn, M. W. (Marianne W.), 1944–
  It's subtraction! / by M. W. Penn.
     p. cm. — (Pebble books. Pebble math)
  Includes bibliographical references and index.
  Summary: "Simple rhyming text and color photographs describe subtraction"—
Provided by publisher.
  ISBN 978-1-4296-6039-6 (library binding)
  ISBN 978-1-4296-7070-8 (paperback)
  ISBN 978-1-4765-9447-7 (saddle-stitch)
  1. Subtraction—Juvenile literature. I. Title. II. Title: It is subtraction! III. Series.
  QA115.P465 2012
  513.2'12—dc22   2011003299

Note to Parents and Teachers

The Pebble Math set supports national mathematics standards
related to algebra and geometry. This book describes and
illustrates subtraction. The images support early readers in
understanding the text. The repetition of words and phrases helps
early readers learn new words. This book also introduces early
readers to subject-specific vocabulary words, which are defined
in the Glossary section. Early readers may need assistance to read
some words and to use the Table of Contents, Glossary, Read More,
Internet Sites, and Index sections of the book.

Printed in China by Nordica.
0613/CA21300978
052013   007408SCH

Table of Contents

Take Away

Ask how many you have left.

Count down. Take away.

Subtract to find the difference.

Minus is what we say.

Use Your Fingers

Use your fingers to keep track

As you count the numbers back:

5 lizards in the sun

    3 lizards jump and run

    5, 4, 3 leaves

    2 lizards in the sun.

Now count back again.

This time, start with 10.

10 books on a shelf,

4 to read by yourself.

10, 9, 8, 7

6 books left on a shelf.

5 - 1 = 4

4 - 1 = 3

How Many Left?

5 cookies in a stack,

Take 1 cookie for your snack.

4 cookies on a plate

Subtract 1 cookie Jerry ate.

Alejandro

Ann

Count the letters in a name.

Subtract the letters in this game.

Alejandro minus Ann?

Find the difference, if you can.

9 letters - 3 letters = 6 letters

20 seashells in the sand.

Take 9 shells away by hand.

If there are 9 shells less,

How many left? Can you guess?

$$20 - 9 = 11$$

16

Joey has 4 licorice sticks.

He won't give Andy 1.

Joey has 4 licorice sticks.

And Andy? He has none!

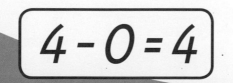

$$4 - 0 = 4$$

18

Mary has 6 apples.

This morning she had 8.

8 minus 6 will tell us

How many Mary ate.

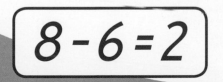

$$8 - 6 = 2$$

Find the Difference

Eat 2 apples or 1 cookie.

Count the lizards as they stray.

See the puppy grab the bone?

Subtract means take away.

Glossary

difference—how many more or less

minus—to take away; a minus sign is shown as −

subtract—to take away

stray—to break away from a group

Read More

Anderson, Jill. *Subtracting with Sebastian Pig and Friends: On a Camping Trip.* Math Fun with Sebastian Pig and Friends! Berkeley Heights, N.J.: Enslow Pub., 2009.

Shaskan, Trisha Speed. *If You Were a Minus Sign.* Math Fun. Minneapolis: Picture Window Books, 2009.

Steffora, Tracey. *Using Subtraction at the Park.* Math around Us. Chicago: Heinemann Library, 2011.

Internet Sites

FactHound offers a safe, fun way to find Internet sites related to this book. All of the sites on FactHound have been researched by our staff.

Here's all you do:

Visit *www.facthound.com*

Type in this code: 9781429660396

Check out projects, games and lots more at
www.capstonekids.com

Index

Word Count: 206
Grade: 1
Early-Intervention Level: 15

Editorial Credits
Gillia Olson, editor; Juliette Peters, designer; Sarah Schuette, photo stylist;
   Marcy Morin, studio scheduler; Laura Manthe, production specialist

Photo Credits
All photos by Capstone Studio/Karon Dubke, except page 20: Shutterstock/Vitaly
Titov & Maria Sidelnikova, 20

The author would like to dedicate this book to Louise Demars, Director of
the New England Carousel Museum.